BUSH
YOGA

BUSH YOGA

DANIEL COTA

BLOOMSBURY

First published in Great Britain 2006

Copyright © 2006 by Daniel Cota

The moral right of the author has been asserted

Bloomsbury Publishing Plc, 36 Soho Square, London W1D 3QY

A CIP catalogue record for this book is available from the British Library

ISBN 0 7475 8934 8
ISBN-13 9780747589341
10 9 8 7 6 5 4 3 2 1

Designed and typeset by John Candell
Printed in China by South China Printing Co

All papers used by Bloomsbury Publishing are natural, recyclable products made from
wood grown in well-managed forests. The manufacturing processes conform to the en-
vironmental regulations of the country of origin.

www.bloomsbury.com
www.bushyoga.com

My fellow Americans, we live in the craziest of times. Across the world, people find themselves living in fear of terrorism, grappling with government corruption, and resenting the repressive rule of religious extremism. It is a good thing that we do not live in such a place.

However, this does not mean that we don't face challenges in our daily lives.

As President of the world's finest democracy, I understand how stressful life can be. The pressures of leadership are many: the five-hour workdays, the foreign policy headaches, constant media access, and a generally reduced amount of fun time are sure to test the strength of any man. How do I deal with it all, you ask? Let me tell you, folks, the ride has not been an easy one. But here, in this book, I have documented the powerful meditation and yoga techniques that allow me to cope with such difficulties. Apply this practice to your daily life and I guarantee you'll see a transformation.

But be warned! With this powerful knowledge comes great responsibility. I am entrusting you to guard it well, and not let it fall into the wrong hands. There are those evildoers who would misuse its power. We must not let this happen.

Now it is time to begin your practice. May you too find that it brings you peace and universal compassion.

Namaste.

George W. Bush

Yoga exercises are known as asanas, yoga postures, or yoga poses. You say "W," I say "Dubya." Whatever makes you happy.

Folks, you know I like to keep things simple, so I've arranged the book into six types of poses:

STANDING POSES

These help you to stand strong; invigorate the mind and body; lend strength and mobility to the hips, knees, neck, and shoulders; and create confidence, enhance willpower, and strengthen character. They are also great poses for increasing your sex appeal.

BALANCING POSES

Balancing postures improve memory and concentration by engaging your whole mind and body. Not my favorites, but still useful.

INVERTED POSES

Inversions change the force of gravity and therefore can reduce signs of aging (like sagging skin). They also ease back pain by relieving stress on the spine and neck, and they help to prevent and alleviate constipation and hemorrhoids. These same benefits can also be had by taking more vacation days. Trust me.

BACK BEND POSES

Back bends bring fresh blood to the head and heart, revitalizing the mind and body. These poses tone the internal organs and glandular system, stimulate brain function, improve circulation, and refresh tired legs. If only you could see how toned my internal organs have become.

SEATED POSES

These poses are considered calming, as they soothe the nerves, eliminate fatigue, refresh the brain, and promote restful sleep. They help me approach each day with brain power at 100%.

RECLINING POSES

Reclining poses serve mainly to stretch the abdomen and increase the mobility of the spine and hips. These are often done at the end of your practice session and help to cool down the body and restore energy. They can be done while sleeping too, which is handy.

Tadasana
Mountain Posture

Commander in Chief on deck! I want you to
take your feet together with your arms to your sides
like you've got yourself two brand-new pistolas. Then,
just stand there, chin up, and think about your favorite
horse. The standing part took me about six months to
master back when I was a C student at Yale. Don't
laugh. It's not so easy after you've knocked back three
bottles of JD.

 This is the starting pose for all standing
poses. Imagine a line of energy all the way up
along your inner thighs to the top of your head.
Make sure not to force your feet together if you have
knock knees.

Adho Mukha Svanasana
Downward-Facing Dog

This little dog pose really makes it easy to
find things that you're looking for. To start, get on your
hands and knees with your toes curled under. Inhale. On
the exhale, push the ground away from you as you lift
your hips up. Focus on finding your keys, WMDs,
personal correspondence with Abramoff, or whatever
you like. I had suggested to Rummy that all the UN
inspectors learn this pose, but those stubborn know-it-
alls never did. Had they taken my advice, I am sure they
would have found what I was looking for.

TIPS Keep your outer arms firm as you press your
fingers and palms into the floor. Your feet
should be hips' width apart with the toes facing
forward. You should feel a stretch at the back of the
legs as you reach your heels toward the floor. If your
back starts rounding, let your knees bend. It is more
important to have your spine long than
it is to have your heels on the ground.
Practice patience.

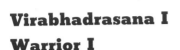

Virabhadrasana I
Warrior I

See here folks, this is a real man's pose.
That must be why I am so good at it! Soldier, what I
want you to do is step forward with your right foot
pointing straight ahead and your back foot turned in
about 45 degrees. Inhale and take your arms up like
you just scored a touchdown for the Longhorns.
Yeehaw! Exhale and bend your front knee. Breathe.

 Line up your heels and ensure that the front
knee is over the front ankle. Make sure your
hips are squared to the front and your tailbone
is tucked. It's okay if your back heel doesn't touch the
floor.

Virabhadrasana II
Warrior II

Now that I know this pose was named after
some warrior who grew from the hair of a blue devil, I
like to use it to strengthen myself against my enemies:
those evildoers who constrict the oxygen supply of
precious freedom. Here's how it's done: I want you to
step forward with your left foot pointing straight ahead
and your back foot turned in about 45 degrees. Inhale
and take your arms out to the side, and on the exhale
bend your front knee. Look past your right hand and
repeat the mantra "God Bless America." This will
counter the evil effects of the pose.

TIPS Draw your shoulder blades toward each other
and down your back. If your arms get tired,
feel free to take your hands to your waist. This
pose is therapeutic for flat feet, osteoporosis, and
sciatica.

Utthita Trikonasana
Extended Triangle

When my mom told me she wanted me to become President, she asked my yogi to explain to me the three branches of the federal government. I remember him saying something about my right shoe being the legislative branch, my left shoe the judicial, and the rest of my body the upward-reaching executive branch. "Kinda like when you're at the ranch and you're thankful for your boots when you step in something awful," I said. He just nodded and smiled at me like he always does.

TIPS You can take your right hand down to your shin instead of the ground. Try to keep a good amount of space between your feet, as the primary focus of the pose should be in the inner groins, hips, and hamstrings. Optional: Picture your trunk turning open and gaze up to the top hand. To release, bend your front leg and push the ground away with your front foot to come up to center. You should not feel strain in your lower back at any time in this pose.

Utthita Parsvakonasana
Extended Sideways Angle

When you do this pose, you will undoob undoubtedbally make this country safer. How? I'm not exactly sure. But I do know that it helps. I can feel it. And I have to tell you, it feels pretty good to know that I am protecting my fellow Americans. All you have to do is step your left foot forward, pointing it straight ahead, with your back foot turned in at a 45-degree angle. Inhale and take your arms out to the side. On the exhale, bend your left knee and place your forearm on your thigh. Then take your right hand and stretch it forward with the palm turned down. Focus your inner mind as if you were clearing away underbrush at the ranch. To release, inhale and reach your right arm up and back down as you straighten the front leg. Mission Accomplished!

TIPS Line up the heels and ensure that the front knee is over the front ankle. You can also perform this pose with your lower arm resting on your bent knee. If you have any neck issue, look straight down at the floor. Do not attempt to look up at your top arm.

Utkatasana
Awkward Chair Pose

Want to know what the toughest part of being President is? Let me tell you folks. It's not meeting all those boring foreign leaders or waking up at night thinking, "Wow, I am the most powerful man in the world." No, with all my public appearances, it's simply not being able to go to the bathroom as much as I used to. It's tough. So, Condi's helped by putting me on a strict bathroom regimen. It usually works great, but when I really need to go, I just do this pose, and then she knows it's urgent. REALLY urgent.

TIPS It may look like you're sitting in an imaginary chair, but there's nothing cushy about this pose. Beginners can work on bringing the thighs closer and more parallel to the floor. For a challenge, bring the hands into a prayer position at the heart and twist to one side. Rest the elbow on the outside of the knee. Don't forget to do the other side.

Prasarita Padottanasana
Wide-Legged Forward Bend

Folks, this really is an easy pose. When I
was a teenager, my daddy told me that I should
probably practice it, and I'm sure glad I did. "Just start
in Tadasana, clasp your hands behind the back, and
bend forward," he said. When the officers stopped me
for that DUI in 1976, they helped me to assume this
position and I astounded them with how well I pulled it
off. I know pride is a sin, but in that moment I just
couldn't help myself.

TIPS Engage the inner parts of your feet and legs
by drawing them up, but make sure not to
lean back into your knees. If you can't bring
your hands to the floor, use a block for support.

★ ★ ★ BALANCING POSES ★ ★ ★ ★ ★

Vrksasana
Tree Pose

Folks, I love this pose because it allows me
to listen to the trees. It's true, and it really works! Last
year I was at the annual Christmas tree lighting and put
myself right into Vrksasana. Then I heard it, "Gmee,
tttrrk mttt." Huh? Rummy was there too and I told him
what I heard. "It is telling us to cut down more trees,"
he said. Of course! I ran to the closest watering hole
and penned the first draft of the Healthy Forests
Initiative. Doing good is too easy sometimes.

 **TIPS** You can use a wall or the cop car for help
initially. Keep the standing knee firm but not
locked. A more advanced option would be to
stretch your arms up to the ceiling with your palms
facing each other to form an inverted V.

Virabhadrasana III
Warrior III

From Tadasana, place your hands together
in front of your chest and lift one foot off the ground.
Then kick that foot behind you as you lean forward like
my favorite teeter-totter at the ranch. When your body
comes about level with the ground, try to straighten
your arms in front of you. To release, bend both knees
and come back to Tadasana. I gotta tell ya, you're
gonna feel so much like Superman (better yet, John
Wayne) that you'll be inspired to fly right into Fallujah
and democratize the country with your trusty six-
shooter.

TIPS Make sure your raised foot, knee, and hip are
all in one line. You can also put your hands at
your heart instead of bringing them forward.
Work to straighten the bottom leg by rooting it through
the ground instead of locking your knee back. Keeping
the navel engaged to the spine will
protect the lower back, but release when
you need to.

Utthita Hasta Padangusthasana
Extended Hand to Big Toe

Hello ladies! Yes, I know that I'm lookin'
pretty good in this pose. Heh, heh. To begin, start in
Tadasana and lift one leg with the knee bent. Grab it
with your hand and pretend like you're doing a slow-
motion karate kick to the head of an anonymous
evildoer. Haiiii-yah! Sometimes I even fly real ones in
from Guantanamo so I can practice. Slow-motion, but
still fun.

TIPS This pose improves balance and coordination
while opening the hips and stretching the
legs. You can use a strap looped around your
foot if you can't reach it with your hand.

Parivrtta Ardha Chandrasana
Reverse Half Moon

Life can be complicated for sure, and that's
why it's good to use this pose whenever you need to
make tough decisions on the field. I remember walking
into Karl Rove's office and seeing him in the PAC. I
tickled his foot, and he giggled (like he always does)
and then said in all seriousness, "Sir, I've decided we
should leak her name." This pose works so well! I
helped him down and then we went out for tamales and
Diet Cokes.

TIPS This pose is great for memory and
concentration and also stretches the upper
back and shoulders. Make sure to be mindful of
any injuries you may have in those areas. Use a block in
between the hand and the floor if you need help.

Salamba Sirsasana I
Supported Head

Some people joke that I was holding Dick's hand during the 9/11 commission meetings. Look here, I'm the President. Not a little kid. And plus, Dick says I'm a big boy now and lets me eat at the grown-up table (sometimes). Now, my fellow Americans, I'm not gonna lie to you (about this): This here pose is no walk in the park. But with a little practice, you can do it just as well as me. My yogi says to focus on the importance of my head and brain while in this pose. "A country cannot prosper without a wise king to guide it, just as a human body cannot prosper without a wise brain to guide it," he tells me. Dang. That sounds pretty good. I wonder what it means.

TIPS Avoid this pose if you have neck problems or high blood pressure, or if you are menstruating. Do not attempt Salamba Sirsasana on your own unless you have practiced this pose with an experienced teacher. Beginners can start by practicing against a wall. Always rest your weight in your forearms, not in your head or neck.

Upavistha Konasana in Sirsasana
Settled Head Angle

Make no mistake, this pose is an integral
part of my No Child Left Behind program. When you've
got so much blood rushin' to your head, you can't help
but get smarter. This pose is a cost-effective way to
increase test scores—no federal funding necessary.
Just get those kids onto their heads! An added benefit
is that it also helps to clear the nasal passages, which
is great, as there is little in this world as frustrating as
the inability to snort things quickly.

TIPS If you feel any pressure on your neck when in
the pose, please come down one leg at a time
as your arms may simply be too short for the
traditional version.

Halasana
Plow

I have always considered the ability to plow forward despite the cautions of the less powerful to be a very admirable quality in a leader. That's why I practice Halasana. To begin, start by lying down. Inhale the legs up and support your lower back with your hands. Let your feet fall behind your head. I've heard that some people may consider me to be headstrong, but let me tell you, I am not nearly as headstrong as I would like to be. Some of my more moderate advisors tell me that I should perhaps reconsider this. After a little Halasana, though, I realize the truth. They are wrong.

TIPS When your toes are on the floor, lift the top of your thighs and tailbone toward the ceiling and draw your inner groins deep into the pelvis. Continue to draw your chin away from your sternum and soften your throat. Use a blanket or a wedge to help you and make sure not to flatten your neck while lifting up the tailbone.

Setu Bandha Sarvangasana
Bridge Pose

Bridges, bridges, bridges. I love bridges.
Almost as much as I love pretzels. Like me, they unite
this fine country, and don't divide. Start in Savasana,
clearing the mind and especially not thinking of
unpleasant things like Ralph Nader. Inhale the thighs
upward. Relax. My yogi tells me to focus on the
Republican and Democratic parties coming together. If
only the Dems would just be more open-minded and
think like me. Then, unity would be so much easier.

TIPS You can modify this pose by interlacing the
hands together behind your back. Walk the
shoulders in and press down with your arms
and shoulders. You can also use a block to support the
hips.

Salabhasana
Locust

Some people think that this pose will
summon a plague of locusts, but that doesn't usually
happen. However, it does help one understand the mind
of the evil locust. Once you understand the locust, you
can predict the actions of evildoers around the world
and bring them to justice. To begin, place yourself in
Salamba Sirsasana with the arms placed further behind
the head. Then, just bend your knees. It is emotionally
demanding work, for sure, but is currently one of my
most effective strategies in the antiterrorism effort.

 You might want to pad the floor below your
TIPS pelvis and ribs with a blanket. Keep your gaze
forward or slightly upward without jutting your
chin forward. Keep the base of your skull lifted and the
neck long.

Urdhva Mukha Svanasana
Upward-Facing Dog

When Dick is mad at me, I sometimes use
this pose to contact the spirit of my dearly departed
dog Spot. He was dang smart, and his foreign policy
advice was the best. To contact the dead pet of your
choice, first lay down and bring your hands under your
shoulders. Exhale and push the floor away from you as
you arch your back and look up. Watch out for your
pubis, though—especially if it is unusually large like
mine. (Remember those candid photos of me in my
flight suit?) Nevertheless, this pose is well worth it.
Finish by lowering yourself down with an inhale.

TIPS If you feel compression in your lower back, do
not straighten your arms or lift your thighs off
the ground. Instead, bend your elbows back and
use the strength of your whole back to arch up. This is
Bhujangasana (Cobra).

Ustrasana
Camel

Saddam. Oh, Saddam! How you haunt my dreams at night! I still remember seeing that photo of you in your underwear. To think, the supreme evildoer of the world wears the same brand as I! I told my yogi about the confusion I felt at seeing such a thing, and he recommended Camel pose. "Start by sitting on the knees, and then grab the ankles and rise up above your jealousy and confusion," he told me. It has definitely helped me, but just to be safe, I've asked Laura to buy me a different brand.

TIPS Your lower ribs shouldn't be protruding toward the ceiling (this will compress your lower back). Turn your elbow creases forward (without squeezing the shoulder blades together). Be careful not to stretch your neck or harden your throat.

Purvottanasana
Inclined Plane

Air Force One is my friend. Whenever I'm
aboard, I make sure to do this Inclined Plane pose at
least five times so that it knows that I'm its friend too.
Start in Savasana and then, exhaling, lift your rump
skyward. Sometimes, I even do this pose on the wing of
the plane when it is grounded. I love Air Force One.
Newsweek took some photos when I was on the wing a
couple weeks ago, but for some reason Dick tells me
that all the shots have been classified. Too bad.

TIPS This is a great core-strengthening exercise.
Once you are aligned from the toes to the
shoulders and it feels good, drop your head all
the way back.

Sukhasana
Easy Pose

Ah, the Xbox pose. I do love this pose!
Whenever I jump into it, Laura knows that I want to
play a little Xbox, and she brings one right over. It's
great at relieving some of the stresses I have
experienced as President. Take, for instance, when my
summer vacation was interrupted by that mom . . . that
soldier's mom. I forget her name, but I can't forget the
anxiety she caused! Here I was trying to cut back some
overgrown trees in peace and all I hear are these
people outside carrying on about . . . something. I don't
even know what! I had no choice but to immediately
jump into Sukhasana and wait for my Xbox. People,
c'mon! Show some respect! I *am* the President of the
United States, you know.

TIPS
You can modify this pose by placing a blanket
under your knees or hip bones. Just sit up and
enjoy the groundedness and inner calm
that this pose provides.

Dandasana
Stick Pose

Okay, boys and girls, this is a boring pose. I know my teacher told me that it's supposed to be some kinda deep meditation thing or something, but even I have my limits. It was hooey like this that kept me out of the classroom. Like my daddy told me, "Inner peace is having your finger on the red button."

TIPS This is the foundation for seated poses, so it's worth trying. Make sure the spine is long and perpendicular to the floor. If your lower spine begins to collapse, sit on a blanket or foam wedge. Turn your gaze past your toes. Imagine the "staff" at your core rooted firmly into the earth while the top of your head reaches toward the sky.

Paripurna Navasana
Boat Pose

Folks, this is a tough pose, to be sure. It strengthens the core, and my yogi tells me that it strengthens the backbone too. I used to do this pose twice a day in the hope that it would increase my courage and allow me to one day complete my National Guard service. Let me tell you folks, that goal was never met, but that doesn't mean I can't "bring the justice" to the evildoers of the world. I hone my skills with my favorite game—Battlefield 2: Special Forces. There really is such a thing as being too good.

TIPS If you are pregnant or menstruating, practice this pose with care or skip it entirely. If you can't stretch your legs, bend your knees and use a strap around the soles of your feet. Allow your spine to round a bit so you feel the work happening in the abdomen.

Upavistha Konasana
Seated Angle

This one is really one of my favorites. I would have never learned it, but the other day I walked into the Oval Office, and Condi and Dick were both on the floor with their legs spread like radar antennae. Dick says the pose makes it easier to find Osama and bring him to justice. Just sit down with your legs as wide apart as you can. Place your hands next to your hips and inhale, lifting your spine tall. Exhale and lean forward. Breathe. Find Osama.

 **TIPS** Don't forget to roll your thighs outward so that the kneecaps point straight up to the ceiling. Make sure to keep your spine long as you bend forward. If your lower back rounds a lot, you can sit on a folded blanket, or better yet, a foam wedge. As always, feel free to use a blanket or a bolster.

Viparita Karani
Inverted Leg Stretch

My yogi refers to this as the "great mother
of all restorative postures," and I think I know why. I
have been in this pose while giving birth to some of my
greatest ideas: war in Iraq, veteran health care
reappropriations, and social security reform.
Sometimes, the depth of my own wisdom frightens me. I
am starting to worry that being this smart might one
day make my brain explode. Luckily, my yogi tells me
that there is no danger of that happening.

TIPS You should feel this pose in the form of a
stretch for your legs. For less of a stretch, you
can rest your legs against a wall. This pose is
good for almost anything that ails you.

Jathara Parivartanasana
Stomach Twist

Believe it or not, but sometimes a stomach twist can be a very good thing. And I'm not talking about the ones that I usually get after sharing dinner with foreign officials. People wonder why I don't like to meet with them. It's the food! Come on, guys, just serve it up Texas-style and I'll be there every week! To twist, lay on your back with your arms to your sides. Inhale your knees into your chest and exhale to take them to one side. Turn your head to the other side and straighten your legs so that your feet might touch your hand. To switch, bend your knees and draw them in with an inhale, then follow the directions for the first side. Did you know this is a liver detoxification pose as well? Lucky for me! After those late nights in the war room, I need all the help I can get.

TIPS You can also do this pose without straightening your legs. Try to soften your gaze and relax the jaw. Do not perform this if you are pregnant.

Anantasana
Reclining Eternal One

Many of you think gas prices are too high. I understand, and that's why I've envisioned a plan to alleviate this situation. While in the middle of a Pentagon briefing (and doing a little Anantasana), it occurred to me that this pose can help solve the oil crisis. To start, just lie on your side and lift one leg skyward. Breathe deeply, and *imagine* us lessening our dependence on Saudi and Iraqi oil. Presto: Down the gas prices go!

 Try to keep your whole body in one line, not rolling to one side or the other. Use a strap around the foot of the lifted leg if you cannot straighten it.

Supta Baddha Konasana
Lying-Down Bound Angle

Ah . . . my own personal freeway to enlightenment. Start in Savasana, then bend the knees and bring up the arms. When I'm on vacation at the ranch, I can usually be found doing a little SBK. Ah . . . I do love this pose. And I'm getting pretty close to enlightenment too. When Hurricane Katrina hit, and FEMA chief Brown burst in on my practice and yelled, "Sir, we have an emergency," I was 94% enlightened. "Brownie," I said . . . heh, heh, I call him Brownie. "Brownie, can't you see I'm busy here? Let's just get back to them in a couple of days."

TIPS If your groin is tight, do not push your knees to the floor. This will only harden the groin (as it will your belly and lower back). Instead, imagine your knees floating up toward the ceiling and continue settling your groin deeper into your pelvis. As your groin drops toward the floor, so will your knees. Use a blanket under your thighs if you need support.

Supta Padangusthasana
Sleeping Big Toe Pose

Some people think time travel is difficult, but they've obviously never done this pose before. Start in Savasana. Breathe deeply. Pull one leg back, like the hand of a clock, slowly using it to calibrate the date of your arrival. Personally, I'm fond of my 2000 inauguration party and go there at least once a week. What a blast! When I'm there, I sometimes tell people that we're going to invade Iraq one day. They start laughing! I tell them not to worry and that if things go astray, I'll just go back in time and fix everything.

 **TIPS** You can make this pose slightly easier by raising the lower leg off the floor a few inches on a block

★ ★

Uttana Padasana
Extended Leg Stretch

My fellow Americans, I urge you to begin
practicing this pose today. Start in Savasana, lifting the
arms and legs upwards. Focus your energy into your
hands and breathe smoothly as laser beams shoot from
your fingertips. I usually aim just an inch above my
toes, but sometimes wind up shooting myself in the foot
(not as painful as you might think).

TIPS Make sure to point the toes back toward the
body. Press the balls of the feet forward while
the outside of the feet rolls back. This will help
the inner thighs roll inward and widen the back of the
legs.

Savasana
Corpse

Folks, this pose may look easy, but it really takes hours and hours of practice to master. You don't just lie there on the ground, but rather relax all the muscles of the body. Then the hardest part: Keep your mind from thinking. My yogi tells me that it's a tough thing for most people to do, but that I have a special knack for it. That makes me happy.

TIPS This pose will conclude your practice and relax your body. In Savasana it is essential that the body be placed in a neutral position. Soften the roof of the tongue, nostrils, and forehead. Let the eyes sink to the back of the head.

You've worked hard; enjoy this delicious resting pose.

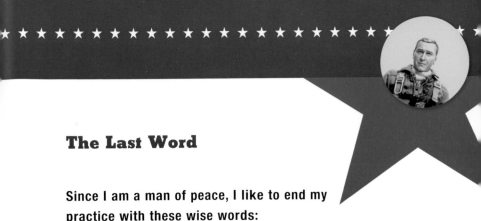

The Last Word

Since I am a man of peace, I like to end my practice with these wise words:

Om shanti shanti shanti

Om is considered to be the sound of the universe, the sound from which all other sounds are formed. "Om" is also a great way to answer a difficult question.

Shanti simply means "peace." I say it three times as I pray for peace individually (like when I can't fall asleep), collectively (when we fight over the last donut at cabinet meetings), and universally (as when I dream of intergalactic democracy).

This book would not have been possible without my mother and father, their parents, and all of our ancestors. I also acknowledge George W. Bush, his family, the American people, the democratic process, luck, fate, social equality, and social inequality for bringing such a catalyzing figure to the American forefront. Also, warm thanks to Joey Huynh (somaticsecrets.com) for his contributions of humorous yoga text, and Blue Box International (blueboxtoys.com) for creating the amazingly flexible George Bush Elite Force Aviator action figure. Thanks as well to my agent, Laura Nolan, for her professionalism and guidance, and to my editors, Yelena Gitlin and Colin Dickerman, for making the whole process so enjoyable. Thanks also to my mom for her advice, Ann for her recommendation, and Rebecca for both her sweetness and inspiration. Last, but not least, here's to Adam and all those in this world who will never give up pursuing what they believe in.

Daniel Cota is an artist and entrepreneur whose collection of Web sites currently draws about 500,000 visitors a year. His most recent project, an experiment in collaborative art, can be found at art.othernet.com. He is currently planning on constructing the world's largest software company, and can sometimes be found singing in and photographing around the San Francisco Bay Area.